DERECHO

by J Matthew Waters

Raw Earth Ink

2021

Published by Raw Earth Ink
PO Box 39332
Ninilchik, AK 99639
www.raw-earth-ink.com

for Judith Mary Doyle

paraphrasing

How can you possibly start a poem now
all things considered

It's true the world is always near the end
but you stay because you simply
must see it for yourself

Frost himself spoke of starting a journey
having no idea where it would take him

And so here we are just as we've
always been
always changing & always finding
new kinds of rhymes & words
in the shadiest of places

You collect them over a lifetime
and you take them with you
in the end

introduction

On August 10, 2020 with very little time to prepare, a derecho hit the City of Cedar Rapids, Iowa, causing widespread devastation throughout the community. The Midwest is known for flooding and tornados, but no one anticipated a fast-moving hurricane-like storm with straight-line winds of up to 140 miles per hours lasting over 45 minutes. The unprecedented storm damaged every corner of the 75 square mile city, impacting every resident in some way. Until that day the term derecho was unknown to most everyone in Cedar Rapids.

When the storm passed and people went outside, they saw their beloved trees laying across lawns and streets. Many homes were devastated, and neighborhoods were unrecognizable. What had taken generations to grow, toppled in minutes. Up to 100,000 trees were damaged and destroyed—more than 65 percent of the city's tree canopy.

The National Oceanic and Atmospheric Administration reported the storm caused $7.5 billion in damage between South Dakota and Ohio, ranking it as the costliest thunderstorm in U.S. history.

Before the storm hit, I was working downtown, a ten-minute drive from my home. Once we realized the power would not be restored anytime soon, we all left for our homes. It took me over an hour to get home because streets were blocked with felled trees. It took some of my coworkers two to three hours to finally reach home. I was unable to reach my house by car but a neighbor down the street allowed me to park in his driveway. By the time I finally arrived my wife and son-in-law were already hauling debris from the back of the house to the street. We lost three blue spruces and two spiral junipers out back and the tall oak in front. A section of the roof had lost its shingles. We were one of the lucky ones with the house largely spared of damage.

We were without power for 13 days, but we got the generator going and managed to keep the refrigerator running. We plugged in the television and watched our reality being played out on the local and national news (I have an outdoor antenna connected to the cabling). I had to travel 30 miles away to get gas for the generator because the gas stations were without power. That lasted a few days. Cellular service was spotty. Nobody had internet service and ours was restored some 30 days later.

As a poetry blogger I write and post an original poem every day. I was not going to allow this derecho from stopping me. Using only my iPhone and my WordPress app I posted a short poem that first night. A few days later my daughter loaned me her iPad which had unlimited data. Creating a hotspot I was able to start using my Chromebook again which made writing and posting much easier. I continued to write and post one poem every night.

The city is still recovering from the derecho, still clearing debris, and hauling away. For me what remains are the poems that follow, all written from the beginning of August through September 3. These poems are not a journal of what happened, but simply reflects my state of mind before and after that fateful day.

losing a whole year

I've seen this before
it's what some call a repeat
déjà vu if you will
like a herd of elephants
lumbering across the sky

I've seen this before
magically recasted to the TV
runners on second & third
the next three batters
striking out looking

I've seen this before
rain falling like stars
washing out the elephants
and delaying the game
probably until next year

home on a sunday

it's six-thirty local time
& I've exhausted
all my free passes
having encircled the globe
these past forty-eight hours
arriving back home
unceremoniously
& empty-handed

exactly what I was expecting
I can't begin to say
but this time I had a feeling
something would be different
like happening upon
a door or a window
only I would be able to open

but no such egress
was in the offing
& now I'm back to the only reality
that I've ever known
planning on accumulating points
for more free passes
thinking next time
things will end differently

midnight in rome

It's midnight in Rome
& nobody knows
what year it is

Writing by candlelight
has become popular of late
encrypted messages
sent all these centuries
the undeliverables
circulating in the periphery

It's midnight in Rome
& a little girl is fast asleep
safely in her second story bedroom
her projected outer self
sitting at the window
receiving & translating
writing feverishly
by candlelight

fueling the fire of creation

we carved him out of an old cedar
all that remained that is
all eight feet tall of him

we kept his arms by his sides
& his chin slightly lifted
his abandoned eyes looking westward
forever waiting for the seven o'clock sun

as we worked together diligently
using chainsaws & assorted knives
the children scrambled feverishly
around his root-like feet
crafting creatures out of clay

after nightfall the squirrels & sparrows
rabbits & foxes & owls & porcupines
[just to name a few]
burned inside the oven of creation
the cedar stretching ever taller
toward a night sky that has no end

starting from scratch

the future was here the day I was born
been working at it ever since
just to keep in step

it doesn't matter what part of the world
you find yourself
explosions may one day come out of
(the proverbial) nowhere

and suddenly you find yourself
back at the beginning
unable to explain to yourself
(or to anyone who may be listening)
how one major blast
can easily wipe out
multiple decades past

the wick effect

cleaning out the garage
on a hot summer's day
dealing with near empty bags
of charcoal & oily rags
gasoline cans & a bale of hay
nearly out of sight & mind

breathe in & breathe out
it's what you do all afternoon
deciding on what gets pitched
& what gets rearranged
all the while contemplating
that first cigarette break

time vs. velocity

afraid I might pass
I've decided I'm not looking
for an easy way out

do you remember
telephones with cords
receiver lying
sideways on the queen
me playing a few chords
on the classical
you singing half-heartedly
sounding just like carly

it was as if you were
in my parent's bedroom
& I was pretending
to be ex-times my age
[repeatedly digressing
into limitless possibilities]
you always asking me
before hanging up
why can't we be like the wind

never in your lifetime

the great experiment proved
to be nothing but a farce
so many years & so many lies
if you want to find the truth
forget about dwelling on the past
instead try looking inwards

with ever greater speed & frequency
history continues to be rewritten
the most recent far from reality
but rest assured eventually
things will be gotten right
unfortunately never in your lifetime

lying for no good reason

the sun stayed behind
the clouds all day long
but the heat
the heat man
it seems that is all they
wanted to talk about

don't go out
don't go out they would say
there's nothing out there for
anyone anymore
but the fact of the matter remains
they're all lying
using every single reason
there is in the book

yeah times are changing
but they always do
this much we know
yeah times are changing
and so are you
sometimes one step
& sometimes
ten thousand steps at a time

straight line winds

straight line winds
is that what you call them
flattening everything in their wake
leaving me & everyone else
without a chance in hell
of making it home before midnight

smoke if you got 'em

I'd smoke if I had 'em
but I kicked that habit
some twenty years ago
I'm just happy I keep
a little weed stashed away

It seems to me
that one god has never
been this angry
or maybe I'm just being a bit selfish
knowing that they murdered
his only son in brutal fashion
back when everything must have been
a little less complicated

reading braille

once the war
was so many years old
the children picked up braille
& began reading again
fairly easily

redirecting local traffic

how far can you open your mind
one in which expands & contracts
at your non-verbal commands
like some non-conformist guru

I've never been challenged
quite like this before
diffusing so many noises
coming from so many directions
tunneling them into a single sound
traveling directly toward me
at thousands of miles per hour

I used to think everything moved
from the west to the east
just like supersonic jet streams
& old familiar trade routes
ones in which you carved yourself
long before you were born again

slow dancing in my peripheral

the power is off
& all the doors are locked
baby's fast asleep upstairs

it's a bit scary tonight
make no mistake
I'm even a little worried
about keeping two candles burning
two battery powered fm radios
on either side of the room
playing damn near in unison
like two old lovers
slow dancing in my peripheral

we've got tonight

offline & uninfluenced by current events
we listen to old vinyls on a powerless night

generator running in every other backyard
sounding like lawn mowers with no place to go

seems like tomorrow can't get here soon enough
but then again there's nothing wrong with tonight

it's just a minor thing

it's been a long time coming
but people are finally reading you
slowly figuring things out in their
own weird way
reiterating yes yes yes
to whatever more you have to say

taking the first train to mexico
somehow became the next reality
thoughts & words left unspoken
dreams suspended
at least for the time being
worlds spinning & maybe colliding

growing grayer by the second

he reminded me of bukowski
or lebowski
I can't remember which
disheveled & maybe talking to himself

but there he was waltzing
through the aisles in his bathrobe
or batman cape
or some such in-or-out-of-fashion thing
dangling a loaf of wonder bread
holding onto a few precious items

somehow he snuck in first
at the wine & spirits checkout
me with my twelve pack
& he with his precious selections
(plus two bags of ice in the minicart)
annoyingly amusing with all that
fumbling for payment options
& mumbling via chit chat about local
sports & the art of social distancing
numerous times checking front left
& back right pockets
the hair on his chinny chin chin
growing grayer by the second

get away

I know Tracy has access to a fast car
but that's not gonna make it for me
I'm thinking there must be a better way

nonetheless she's in the background
singing the same song in a different key
comforting me when I need it most
reminding me there's always another way

yeah I've got a job that pays all the bills
but I'm thinking working for a living
can get you only so far
that driving a fast car is fun for awhile
unless of course you can make it fly

but in reality it never really was

my dream is your reality
revisiting things that could have been
unable to change the course of events
but getting plenty of food for thought
be they apples or bananas
growing abundantly from utility poles
repurposed so many years ago

this place is not what it used to be
but in reality it never really was
& the minute you think
you've got everything figured out
something stranger comes marching on
making it perfectly clear
you're no longer the new kid in town

not guilty

I heard she'd contracted the virus
& it wasn't just hearsay
was told she drove 80 miles to Waterloo
to find out if it was true

god knows how long that will take

we may never know the results
having packed our bags
heading in the opposite direction
cell phones no longer working
& no destination in mind
just a strange idea that being on the move
is somehow better than doing nothing at all

each time we stop for supplies
I casually pick out meaningless postcards
compile them into the glovebox
foolishly thinking one day
I'll turn them into something special

wishing upon a star

we'd become separated by no fault of our own
unable to remember if it was due to gunfire
or mother nature herself

out back the horses are long gone
having escaped before the doors swung shut
galloping faster than the wind
their hooves barely touching the ground

from what I've learned things may never die down
& those stars shining ever brighter
will one night once again be wished upon

burying the past

the game's over
it's taken me more years than expected
to make it all the way back home

I'd been fighting
for so many lives than my own
when they finally brought me back
I was not going to burden anyone

I was going to do what I've always done
determined to show
strength comes from different places

eventually I had to face the reality of my own
a little box less than five feet tall
steel capped boot pressing shovel
repeatedly into the earth

check one-two-three

my heart's once again
connected to the outside world
beating irregularly
sending mixed signals
online & offline & back online again
sometimes unsuspecting angels
come in & take a look
but only when they have time

in my mind
I'm back in the garage
putting the improvised band
back together again
working my rock star drum kit
in an attempt to attract
rising or fading stars
willing to give it another shot

inside the eye of the storm

make-believe people ask me
what was I thinking
when everything went down

I just smile like an idiot
having never been blown away
by such a bout of reality

if I was thinking I'd probably
have done things differently
maybe pretend I was a reporter
jotting down some notes
or voice recording objectively
what it was I was witnessing

instead I found myself swirling
inside the eye of the storm
past & present souls gathering
aiding & abetting my inner strength

minority bill of rights

I dreamed in a prior life
we spoke another language
the strangest of worlds
becoming all too familiar

there is this other place
far away from home
where certain spoken words
take on greater meaning

intuitively we are drawn
chasing what is ours
whether intrinsically so
or rightfully speaking

business as usual

I've neglected my hummingbird friends
far too long but through no fault of my own
oh how they must be a forgiving sort
returning once finding me back on my feet

it's true the natural nectar may have been
decimated by the wicked wicked winds
but now there is sunlight to be found
between blinking eyes & barren ground

it's true the landscape is ever changing
leading us to say we live in interesting times
though matter of factly it's business as usual
reaching out & routinely replenishing

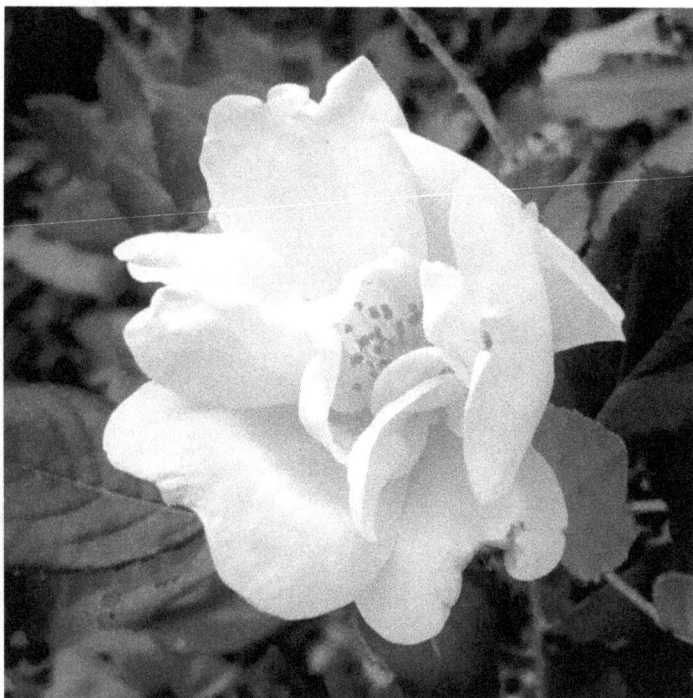

just a phase

it was a billy joel kind of morning
the big hand crossing over six
she's always a woman playing on the a-side
soon to flip over to anthony's song

in the old days you'd make a racket
demanding I clock in as the doorman
before I was good & ready
even before the first song ever ended

over time your musical tastes changed
right along with mine
lately banging our heads against the door
reluctant to find what's on the other side

seven bullets

this is not the same place it used to be

the neighborhood
the municipality
the county & the state
and all those interconnected

yes there are safe zones & hot spots
but they can flip on a dime
and then where will you be
either in the safest place imaginable
or right there in the middle of the fray

I used to call them the police
but now I'm finding myself calling them cops
like I did when I was a little kid
when we played cops & robbers
running unrestrained between houses
and through back alleyways
taking to the safety of the park
and all its beaten paths & tallest pines
doing my damndest to shake them
as they close in within earshot
suddenly emptying half their round
without even a warning

toxicity

I'm all alone in my room
listening to toxicity
unfamiliar lyrics
forming & shaping
my current state of mind
drinking casually
drawing smoke to my lungs
needle & spoon
within arm's reach

I sing along whenever I can
guessing what words
may come next
as if learning a new language
the recording progresses
banging my head
against an imaginary wall
thrashing my head
into the electrified air

the fortitude & the will

choose wisely what you remember
if that is even possible

despite the accuracy of the moment
the further back you go
the more vivid it seems to be

there is an aum in your future
I can feel it
one in which forces you to slow
things down
opening the possibility
of moving further
than you've gone thus far
in your short time here

from there you can launch yourself
as long as you continue to possess
the fortitude & the will

three weeks after

the season is quickly changing
and most of the houses
are dark by 8pm

it's hard to say how many
are abandoned
voluntarily or otherwise

the streets are littered with what
the winds left behind
there's hardly any room
for any kind of truck to pass through

the smell of mixed wood abounds
whether freshly cut
or burning miles away
hundreds of wood chip pyramids
magically appear overnight

the carnival was supposed to be in town
(a fresh change from
all the other outsiders)
but it was abruptly cancelled
just like everything else

undoing the end of time

I imagine as the years pass
change appears to quicken its pace
when in fact all along it's been this way
from the very start

people are passionate by nature
though by many varying degrees
hiders & seekers alike
attempting to vainly save themselves
or selflessly saving others

we can stampede much faster
than one or twenty horses
kicking up dirt & turning the landscape
into a horizontal blur
or methodically slow things down
to a virtual crawl
wiping clear the skies & undoing
the end of time

an ordinary world

tanks rolling through town
escorting a larger entourage
little legs running right along
keeping up with the pace
robotic machines with long legs & long arms
marching & singing 'one two three four
who are we fighting for'

everything's been canceled
the parade is all there is
children singing 'one two three four'
lighting snakes & small fires by the curbside
strategizing about stargazing
wildly boasting of shooting the moon
and bringing down the sun god

isolated & medicated

nobody really knows what happened
just like nobody knows what will

they keep saying something bad
is bound to happen to him
but it never does

in the meantime we are picking up
all kinds of pieces
large & small & medium & minuscule
picking up the tiniest shards of glass
(slightly larger than molecules)
grinding them to nothing with our teeth

this town used to be something
nearly opposite than it is today
medicated & isolated
its people slowly turn on themselves
for explanations unimaginable

about the author

J MATTHEW WATERS was born on November 13, 1961 in Rock Island, Illinois, but grew up across the Mississippi in Davenport, Iowa. He graduated from the University of Iowa in 1984 with a B.A. in English. His latest poetry efforts can be found at jdubqca.com.

other books by J Matthew Waters

Five Hundred Pieces
In the Middle of Somewhere
101 Chances
Forty-five Revolutions per Minute
Thirty Days Before May

www.ingramcontent.com/pod-product-compliance
Lightning Source LLC
Chambersburg PA
CBHW021921040426
42448CB00007B/856